THE WORLD'S GREATEST
TRUCKS AND EARTHMOVERS

Ian Graham

Raintree

www.raintreepublishers.co.uk
Visit our website to find out more information about Raintree books.

To order:
 Phone 44 (0) 1865 888112
Send a fax to 44 (0) 1865 314091
Visit the Raintree Bookshop at www.raintreepublishers.co.uk to browse our catalogue and order online.

First published in Great Britain by Raintree, Halley Court, Jordan Hill, Oxford, OX2 8EJ, part of Harcourt Education.
Raintree is a registered trademark of Harcourt Education Ltd.

Editorial: Andrew Farrow and Dan Nunn
Design: Ron Kamen and Philippa Baile
Picture Research: Hannah Taylor and Elaine Willis
Production: Duncan Gilbert

Originated by Dot Gradations Ltd.
Printed in China

The paper used to print this book comes from sustainable resources.

ISBN 1 844 21266 1
10 09 08 07 06
10 9 8 7 6 5 4 3 2 1

British Library Cataloguing in Publication Data
Graham, Ian, 1953-
  Trucks and earthmovers. – (The world's greatest)
  1. Trucks – Juvenile literature
  2. Earthmoving machinery – Juvenile literature
  I. Title
  629.2'24
A full catalogue record for this book is available from the British Library.

Acknowledgements
The publishers would like to thank the following for permission to reproduce photographs:

Bert Visser Dredgers p. **25**; Corbis pp. **4** (Craig Aurness), **5 top** (Lester Lefkowitz), **5 bottom** (Sandro Vannini), **8** (Reuters/Tim Wimborne), **9** (Bennett Dean/Eye Ubiquitous), **10** (Ed Kashi); Komatsu pp. **16**, **17 top**, **17 bottom**, **22**; LeTourneau Inc pp. **14**, **15**; Leibherr France SAS pp. **1**, **12**, **13**, **24**; Man Takraf pp. **18**, **19**; O&K pp. **20**, **21**; Oshkosh p. **11**; P&H Mining Equipment p. **23**; Peterbilt p. **6**; Volvo pp. **7 top**, **7 bottom**.

Cover photograph reproduced with permission of ATM Images.

Every effort has been made to contact copyright holders of any material reproduced in this book. Any omissions will be rectified in subsequent printings if notice is given to the publishers.

Contents

Words appearing in the text in bold, **like this**, are explained in the Glossary.

Trucks and earthmovers

Trucks are vehicles that carry all the things we eat, wear, and use. Trucks transport raw materials to factories to make things like clothes and toys. Trucks also carry these things from the factories to shops. They transport food from farms to factories and shops too.

Off-road giants

Most of the trucks we see are on roads. But huge trucks and digging machines also work at mines and construction sites. They move large amounts of earth, coal, and rock. Trucks that use roads have to fit in with other vehicles. Big diggers and earthmovers don't travel on public roads. They can be much bigger than road trucks. Some of them are giant vehicles.

Trucks transport goods and materials all over the country.

Trucks and earthmovers move huge amounts of coal, earth, and rock out of mines.

Trucks carry produce from farms to markets. They also move goods to towns and villages.

The greatest road trucks

Trucks have to carry heavy loads for long distances. They need powerful engines. The biggest trucks on our roads are called big rigs in the United States, artics in Britain, and semis in Australia.

These big trucks have two parts. The front part with the engine is called the tractor. The tractor is then connected to a semi-trailer. This lets the truck bend in the middle. It also lets a tractor unhook a load and pick up another load quickly and easily.

The Peterbilt Model 379 is a long-nosed big rig. It is used throughout the United States and Canada.

semi-trailer

tractor

Trucks with flat fronts are more common in Europe than in the United States. They are called cabovers. The driver sits above the engine.

Types of trucks

Some trucks are made to carry one type of cargo. For example, tanker trucks carry liquids such as milk, oil, and petrol. Refrigerated trucks keep fresh food cold. Car transporters carry cars on a special double-deck trailer.

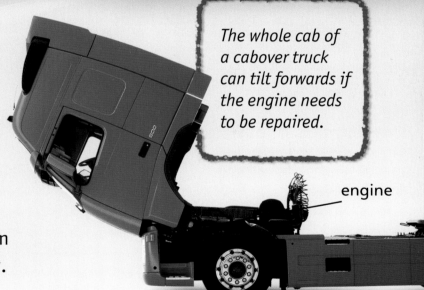

The whole cab of a cabover truck can tilt forwards if the engine needs to be repaired.

engine

Peterbilt Model 379 'big rig' truck

BMW 316i family car

	Peterbilt Model 379 'big rig' truck	BMW 316i family car
Engine:	14.6 litres/891 cu in	1.8 litres/110 cu in
Power:	up to 625 horsepower	115 horsepower
Weight:	36.3 tonnes fully loaded	1.3 tonnes

A big rig with a full load weighs as much as 28 cars.

The longest road trucks

The longest trucks in the world drive up and down Australia's dusty roads. They are called road trains. Most Australians live in a few cities around the coast. Goods have to be moved great distances between these cities. This is done by road trains.

Prime movers

Most road trains have a tractor, called the prime mover. This pulls three or four trailers. Some road trains are even longer. Each trailer is as long as three cars. This is a very heavy load to pull, so prime movers of road trains are far more powerful than most truck tractors.

Road trains like this one move goods all over Australia.

LONG VEHICLE
A road train with three trailers is as long as 11 cars.

Don't run out of fuel!

There are very few **fuel** stations on the long roads in Australia. Road trains carry enough fuel for about 1,600 kilometres (1,000 miles). They often travel in groups called convoys. This is so a road train that breaks down always has help nearby.

Australian road train

Length:	**53 m/174 ft**
Trailers:	**3**
Load pulled:	**140 tonnes**
Engine power:	**650 horsepower**
Speed:	**100 kph/60 mph**

Road trains have strong bars across the front. The bars protect them from damage if they hit a wild animal. The bars are called bull bars, but drivers are more likely to find kangaroos than bulls on the road!

The biggest army movers

Armies have to move lots of heavy equipment, such as tanks. They need big, powerful trucks. The biggest trucks used by the army are the Oshkosh HETs. HET stands for Heavy Equipment Transporter.

The super-trailer

The HET is a powerful tractor unit. It pulls special military trailers. The trailers have ramps at the back that can be lowered for loading vehicles. Up to 40 wheels share their heavy weight over the road. Some of the wheels turn to steer the trailer when the driver turns the tractor's steering wheel.

The HET's main job is to take tanks and other military vehicles to wherever the army needs them.

Tank transporter

The Oshkosh HET carries tanks such as the American Abrams tank. Each of these fearsome battle tanks weighs as much as 50 cars! The HET can carry other heavy loads too, such as **artillery** guns and armoured cars. It can travel by road or cross rough ground. The front and back wheels steer to help it get round tight turns.

The HET has to go wherever the army needs it. Sometimes there are no roads to get there.

Oshkosh 1070F HET

Engine:	**700 horsepower diesel**
Weight:	**44.9 tonnes**
Fully loaded weight:	**118 tonnes**
Speed (carrying a tank):	**48 kph/30 mph**

The biggest dump truck

The biggest trucks do not drive on public roads. They carry away the earth and rock from mines and construction sites. These huge trucks are called **dump trucks**. The biggest dump truck is the Liebherr T-282B.

Ultra trucks

The T-282B is so high that the driver needs a ladder to reach the cab. It is so wide and long that the driver has to use video cameras to see all round it! The T-282B can carry nearly 25 times more earth than a small dump truck that goes on a public road. Trucks like the T-282B are so big that they are also called Ultra Trucks. The word 'ultra' means beyond or extreme.

A Liebherr T-282B with a full load is so heavy that the ground shakes as it rumbles past.

The trouble with engines

The T-282B has a **diesel engine**, but the engine doesn't drive the wheels! Ultra trucks like the T-282B use their engines like this:

1. A diesel engine drives a **generator**.
2. The generator makes electricity.
3. The electricity powers electric motors. These drive the wheels.

The T-282B can carry more than 360 tonnes of earth.

	Liebherr T-282B	**'15-ton' dump truck**
Length:	14.5 m/47 ft 6 in	7.7 m/25 ft 3 in
Width:	8.8 m/28 ft 10 in	2.5 m/8 ft 2 in
Height:	7.4 m/24 ft 3 in	3.1 m/10 ft 2 in
Engine:	3,650 horsepower diesel	340 horsepower diesel
Load carried:	363 tonnes	15 tonnes
Loaded weight:	592 tonnes	26.2 tonnes

The largest loaders

Sometimes piles of earth and rock on top of the ground have to be cleared away. Earthmovers called loaders do this job. The biggest loader is the LeTourneau L-2350. It can lift a bucket full of earth that weighs more than 50 cars! It can lift the load as high as four men standing on each other's shoulders.

LeTourneau L-2350 Loader

Engine:	2,300 horsepower diesel
Weight:	262.2 tonnes
Bucket load:	72.1 tonnes

Giant loaders like the L-2350 have enormous tyres. The deep **grooves** in the tyres help them to grip the ground.

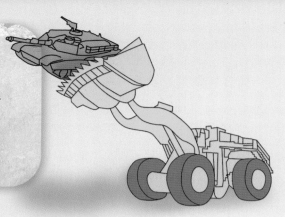

Scooping earth

The L-2350 has to scoop up a lot of earth. It has a wide bucket at the front. The vehicle drives towards the pile of earth and pushes the bucket into it. The bucket is lifted up. It is also tilted back so that nothing falls out. It has to be lifted high enough to go over the top of a dump truck. Then the bucket is tilted down and the earth falls into the truck.

The biggest loaders are designed to load the biggest trucks as fast as possible.

The biggest bulldozer

Bulldozers move earth by pushing it. This is called dozing. The bulldozer has a blade at the front. This pushes the earth along.

Super-Dozer

The biggest bulldozer is the Komatsu D575A. This is so big and powerful that it is sometimes called a Super-Dozer. It can move more earth at one time than any other bulldozer. It is more than twice as big and heavy as the world's biggest army tanks.

blade

The Super-Dozer's blade can be lowered or raised. It is lowered to scrape up more earth. It is raised to push less earth.

Komatsu D575A Super-Dozer

Engine:	1,050 horsepower diesel
Weight:	152.6 tonnes
Blade width:	7.4 m/24 ft 3 in
Blade height:	3.2 m/10 ft 6 in

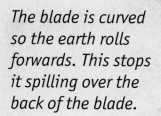

The blade is curved so the earth rolls forwards. This stops it spilling over the back of the blade.

Staying on track

Bulldozers run on **tracks** instead of wheels. Tracks spread their weight over more ground. This stops them sinking into soft earth. Tracks also grip the ground well. This means that bulldozers can push heavy piles of earth.

BIG BLADE

The blade on the front of the Komatsu D575A is as long as two cars. It is more than twice as high too.

ripper

Some bulldozers have a metal spike or hook at the back. This is called a ripper. The ripper is used to break up hard ground.

The greatest land vehicle

The greatest vehicle that travels on land is a giant earthmover. It makes all other trucks and earthmovers look tiny.

A giant among giants

The MAN TAKRAF RB293 is a bucket wheel **excavator** that digs coal out of the ground in Germany. It is not only the biggest earthmover. It is also the biggest land machine that can move under its own power. It is as tall as the Statue of Liberty in New York, and weighs more than 10,000 cars.

The bucket wheel hangs from the end of an arm. This is called a boom. When the boom is lowered the buckets cut into the ground.

boom

bucket wheel

Scooping up coal

The giant excavator works by pushing a huge wheel into the ground. The wheel has buckets all around it. As the wheel turns, the buckets cut into the ground and scoop up the coal. Each bucket is as big as a car!

As the wheel turns further, the coal spills out and lands on a **conveyor belt**. The moving belt carries it away. The RB293 can dig 40,000 buckets of coal in a day.

MAN TAKRAF RB293

Type:	Bucket wheel excavator
Length:	220 m/722 ft
Height:	94.5 m/310 ft
Wheel diameter:	21.6 m/71 ft
Weight:	14,196 tonnes

The RB293 excavator moves on 8 crawlers. It cuts a huge trench through the ground.

The largest hydraulic excavator

Another huge earthmover is the Terex O & K RH400. It has a bucket on a long arm. It uses this to dig and scoop up earth. An experienced operator can move its bucket fast. It takes only about one minute to fill a giant dump truck with three bucket-loads of earth. Each bucket-load of earth scooped up by the RH400 weighs as much as 63 cars.

*The RH400 is the largest **hydraulic** excavator in the world. It has tubes called hydraulic rams. Pumping oil into a ram pushes a rod out of one end. This moves the digger's mechanical arm.*

Giant crawler

The RH400 moves on crawler tracks, like a tank. It travels only short distances around a mine. When an RH400 had to be moved 43 kilometres (27 miles) to another mine in Wyoming, in the United States, it had to be carried there. Eight trailers were joined together to make a platform big enough for the excavator. The trailers had a total of 260 wheels. The excavator was moved so slowly and carefully that the journey took three weeks!

Terex O & K RH400

Type:	Hydraulic excavator
Weight:	980 tonnes
Engine power:	4,400 horsepower
Bucket-load:	85 tonnes

The RH400 is operated by two small hand controllers, like games joysticks.

Other big diggers

One of the world's biggest diggers is the giant Komatsu PC8000. The Komatsu PC8000 is built for mining. Its bucket can scoop up enough earth to fill 117 bathtubs! It can move around at walking pace on two huge crawler tracks. PC8000s are used in mines all over the world.

The PC8000 is so big that the driver sits as high as the third floor of a building

	Komatsu PC8000	P & H 4100XPB
Type:	Hydraulic excavator	Cable-operated excavator
Power:	4,020 horsepower	7,900 horsepower
Weight:	725.7 tonnes	1,400 tonnes
Bucket-load:	68 tonnes	104 tonnes

Speedy digger

The PC8000 is tiny compared to the much bigger P & H 4100XPB. It digs coal in a mine in Wyoming, in the United States. The 4100XPB is called a cable-operated excavator, because its bucket hangs on the end of cables. The machine can move its bucket fast. It can scoop up earth and rock weighing more than 75 cars and drop them into a truck in less than 29 seconds.

The 4100XPB is so big that it has to be transported in pieces. It takes three months to put all the pieces together.

Big backhoes

A digging machine can use its bucket to dig in two different ways. It can push the bucket away from it, like a shovel. Or, it can pull the bucket back towards it, scooping up earth on the way. A bucket that is pulled towards a digger is called a **backhoe**.

The Liebherr 996 can be fitted with a shovel or a backhoe. In this photo, it is fitted with a backhoe.

Digging trenches

Backhoes are good for digging trenches. They can dig down deeper than shovels. Some giant diggers can be fitted with a backhoe instead of a shovel. The Liebherr 996 is one of the biggest.

Floating diggers

Most backhoes are used on dry land, but some float on barges. They clear gravel and mud from the bottom of harbours and water channels. This allows ships to sail through safely. Digging under water like this is called dredging.

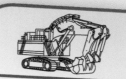

Liebherr R996 Litronic

Type:	Hydraulic excavator
Power:	3,000 horsepower
Weight:	668 tonnes
Backhoe bucket-load:	58.8 tonnes
Shovel load:	60.6 tonnes

This Liebherr 996 floats on a barge in New York harbour. Its backhoe digs 17 metres (nearly 56 feet) below the water to deepen the harbour for ships.

Facts and figures

There are hundreds of trucks and earthmovers. Some of the biggest and most powerful are listed here. You can use the information to see which can move the most earth or carry the heaviest loads. If you want to learn more about these or other trucks and earthmovers, look on pages 30 and 31. There you can find out how to do some research.

Road truck tractors

Name	Engine	Horsepower	Tractor weight	Truck weight (loaded)
Mack CX600 Vision	12 litres/732 cu in	460 horsepower	15 tonnes	36.3 tonnes
Peterbilt Model 379	14.6 litres/891 cu in	up to 625 h.p.	14.9 tonnes	36.3 tonnes
Scania T144L	14.2 litres/867 cu in	530 horsepower	19 tonnes	36.3 tonnes
Western Star 4964SX	14.6 litres/891 cu in	355 horsepower	14.9 tonnes	36.3 tonnes

Dump trucks

Name	Power	Payload	Loaded weight
Caterpillar 797	3,224 horsepower	326 tonnes	557.8 tonnes
Liebherr T-282B	3,650 horsepower	363 tonnes	592 tonnes

Special trucks

Name	Type of vehicle	Power	Loaded weight
Oshkosh 1070F HET	Military transporter	700 horsepower	118 tonnes
Western Star Constellation 4964EX	Australian road train	650 horsepower	140 tonnes

Diggers and earthmovers

Name	Type of vehicle	Weight	Power	Bucket load
Big Muskie	Dragline excavator	12,000 tonnes	62,600 horsepower	300 tonnes
Komatsu D575A	Bulldozer	152.6 tonnes	1,050 horsepower	96.3 tonnes *
Komatsu PC8000	Hydraulic excavator	725.7 tonnes	4,020 horsepower	68 tonnes
LeTourneau L-2350	Front-end loader	262.2 tonnes	2,300 horsepower	72.1 tonnes
Liebherr R996	Hydraulic excavator	668 tonnes	3,000 horsepower	60.6 tonnes
MAN TAKRAF RB293	Bucket wheel excavator	14,196 tonnes	Unknown	Unknown
P & H 4100XPB	Cable-operated excavator	1,400 tonnes	7,900 horsepower	104 tonnes
Terex O & K RH400	Hydraulic excavator	980 tonnes	4,400 horsepower	85 tonnes
The Captain	Power shovel	12,700 tonnes	21,000 horsepower	245 tonnes

* The amount of earth the bulldozer's blade can push.

Big Muskie

The biggest single-bucket digging machine ever built was called Big Muskie. It was a **dragline excavator**. Big Muskie started work in 1969 in the United States. It was as tall as a 22-storey building. It weighed 12,000 tonnes – that's as much as thirty 747-400 Jumbo Jet airliners! Its bucket was big enough to park 12 cars inside. Big Muskie didn't have wheels or crawler tracks. Instead, it walked on huge feet. Big Muskie was shut down for the last time in 1991.

The Captain

The biggest stripping shovel ever made was called the Captain. A stripping shovel is a digger used in a strip mine. A strip mine is a mine where the coal or other valuable material is just below the surface. The Captain was so big that trucks could drive underneath it while it was working. It weighed nearly 13,000 tonnes. It dug coal in Illinois, in the United States, from 1965. It was destroyed by fire in 1991.

Glossary

artillery large army weapon that fires exploding shells. It is also called a field gun.

backhoe bucket on a digging machine that is lowered onto the ground and pulled back towards the machine

conveyer belt an moving loop or band, used to move material from place to place

cu in cubic inch. A space that is one inch long, high, and wide. The space inside an engine where the fuel is burned is sometimes measured in cubic inches (cu in).

diesel engine engine that burns diesel oil. Most trucks and earthmoving machines have diesel engines.

dragline excavator type of digging machine. It lowers a bucket onto the ground and uses cables to pull it along and fill it up.

dump truck truck that tips up. The earth or rock piled up inside it slides out through the **tailgate**. Dump trucks are also called tipper trucks.

excavator another name for a digging machine

fuel substance that is burned in an engine to power a truck. Most trucks have diesel engines. They burn a fuel called diesel oil.

generator a machine that makes electricity

groove channel cut into something. Deep grooves in truck tyres help them to grip soft ground.

horsepower the power of an engine

hydraulic worked by liquid. Hydraulic digging machines move their mechanical arms by pumping oil into tubes called rams. This makes the rams extend, causing the mechanical arms to move.

tailgate back end of a truck. Some dump trucks and tipper trucks have a tailgate that can be unlocked. When the back of the truck tips up, the tailgate swings open. The load then slides out onto the ground.

tracks metal belts, like flattened bicycle chains, that go round a bulldozer's wheels. Tracks spread a bulldozer's weight more evenly over the ground and help it grip the earth.

Finding out more

You can find out more by looking for other books to read and searching the internet.

Books

Here are some more books about trucks and earthmovers:

Mega Book of Trucks (Chrysalis Children's Books, 2004)

Wild About: Trucks and Diggers, by Caroline Bingham (Ticktock Media, 2003)

Young Machines: Trucks, by H. Castor (Usborne Publishing, 2004)

Trucks and earthmovers online

These web sites give more information about trucks and earthmovers:

http://www.kenkenkikki.jp/e_index2.html – visit this web site to find out lots of interesting information about all sorts of construction machines.

http://science.howstuffworks.com/backhoe-loader.htm – this web site looks in detail at how a backhoe digger works.

More to do

New trucks and earthmovers are being built all the time. See what you can find out about them. Look at the web sites run by the biggest manufacturers. These include Mack Trucks, Freightliner, Peterbilt, Kenworth, Caterpillar, and Komatsu.

See if you can find out what was the strangest thing that ever appeared in the bucket of the giant excavator called Big Muskie. Was it:
◎ a dinosaur skeleton?
◎ a school marching band?
◎ a flock of sheep?
(Answer on page 32.)

Trucks and earthmovers of the past

How do you think today's trucks and earthmovers compare to the vehicles used in past times? Were older trucks smaller or bigger than trucks today? Were they slower or faster? Famous trucks of the past include the Ford TT 1-tonner, which dates from 1917, and the Terex Titan of the 1970s.

You can also find information about record-breaking trucks and earthmovers at:
http://guinnessworldrecords.com

Disclaimer
All the Internet addresses (URLs) given in this book were valid at the time of going to press. However, due to the dynamic nature of the Internet, some addresses may have changed, or sites may have changed or ceased to exist since publication. While the author and Publishers regret any inconvenience this may cause readers, no responsibility for any such changes can be accepted by either the author or the Publishers.

Index

Answer to question on page 31

The strangest thing to appear in the bucket of the giant Big Muskie excavator was a school marching band. The bucket was big enough for the band to perform inside it!

Titles in the *The World's Greatest...* series include:

Hardback   1-844-21262-9

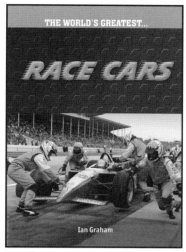

Hardback   1-844-21263-7

Hardback   1-844-21264-5

Hardback   1-844-21265-3

Hardback   1-844-21266-1

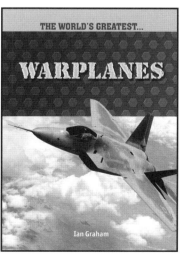

Hardback   1-844-21267-X

Find out about other titles from Raintree on our website www.raintreepublishers.co.uk